VICTORIAN NEWS FROM TOTNES

Short original news reports
which recounted events and
everyday life in Totnes

TODD GRAY

VICTORIAN
NEWS FROM
TOTNES

Short original news reports
which recounted events and
everyday life in Totnes

TODD GRAY

THE
MINT
PRESS

First published in Great Britain by The Mint Press, 2001

ISBN 1-903356-16-4

Cataloguing in Publication Data
CIP record for this title is available from the British Library

The Mint Press
18 The Mint
Exeter, Devon
England EX4 3BL

Text and cover design by Delphine Jones

Cover illustration, Totnes, 1833, courtesy of Westcountry Studies Library

Printed and bound in Great Britain
by Short Run Press Ltd, Exeter.

Foreword

*N*ews flows through our lives like a river rushes through a weir. These days we're better at speeding it on its way and directing it where we want but its content remains reassuringly down to earth and human. It's history in the making, a development by development record of all our lives and the places in which we live them.

This book captures more than sixty years of that river flow, chronicling the lives of many of our predecessors in this distinctive and long-lived town of Totnes. All the glorious colour, triviality, tragedy and sheer gossip of the Victorian generations who inhabited the banks of the River Dart are here.

To read reports of events described in locations as familiar today as they were 150 years ago somehow makes you warm to a place that has provided the backdrop to so many lives.

From the near-death-by-collision-with-crinoline incident on the High Street to the real-death-from-explosion-of-a-locomotive-boiler-tragedy – all life was here then as it is today. The book is replete with fascinating, amusing, pompous and tragic accounts of life in this remarkable town. And for a relatively small population, the number of near disasters seems extraordinary if not a little disconcerting. From the tricycle pile up in Bridgetown, in which an unfortunate rider seems to have been rear-ended, literally, to the dramatic rescue from drowning of a member of the Dart Rowing Club.

This book is a delightful selection of past journalism from an age of English certainty and self-confidence. Those reports and the story they tell of the history of Totnes go some way to explain this intriguing town today with its remarkably broad mix of people and its vibrancy and tolerance.

Richard Bath

TOTNES, 15 SEPTEMBER

Introduction

*T*he rise of the popularity of local newspapers largely coincided with the beginning of the Victorian Age. In Devon these nineteenth-century newspapers included *The Western Luminary, The Exeter Flying Post, The Devon Weekly Times, The Western Times* and *The Devonshire Chronicle*. For the first time daily events and other happenings in localities throughout Devon were regularly reported to readers throughout the county and beyond. Victorian Totnes was one such place that had a frequent short news column. This book reprints some of those reports, forming a selection which is intended to provide an impression of what life was like in the town or at least in how it was represented in the popular press.

The first and last accounts are concerned with the reign of Queen Victoria – the first concerns the celebrations held to mark her coronation in 1838 and the last is a report on the local events that marked her death in 1901.

Some of the reports were meant to amuse and others to inform but many show obvious bias even with the celebrations regarding the Queen's coronation. This is particularly self-evident from the reports of the late 1830s and 1840s that detailed the electoral struggles between the Reformers and the Tories. They represent the town as highly divided and indeed great efforts were made to win the two Parliamentary seats. But finally rumours of bribery and corrupt practices helped to end Totnes having two MPs: the 1865 election was the last in the town after more than 250 years.[1]

The importance of the railway to the town is clearly

seen but many of the reports recorded aspects of more every-day life such as weather, fires, the annual Races, meetings of various local government officials, happenings on the river including reports of salmon caught and the regularity of the steamer service to Dartmouth, and the celebrations on the 5th of November, at Christmas and New Year. Some reports were more sombre such as the notes of justice meted out to those accused and found guilty of crime, the continual concerns over sanitary conditions and the incidence of disease, and a report in 1872 regarding an attempt to establish a union of shoemakers. There were also curious reports: a drunken ventriloquist was accused of disrupting a chapel service and there was a serious, but odd, tricycle accident at Bridgetown. Other events show how fashions and sensibilities change: it is unlikely that the `Ethiopian Serenaders' or 'Nigger Minstrels' will ever again perform in Totnes let alone receive such ecstatic reviews.

In 1840 *Robson's Directory* noted that Totnes 'consists chiefly of one lone street, terminating on the east by a handsome modern bridge, erected about 1827, and connecting Totnes with Bridgetown Pomeroy. Owing to the improvement of the roads, the town is fast increasing, many houses and villas have been built on the Plymouth Road, gas works have been established and various modern alterations have taken place'. By the end of the century the population rate had slowed and the town began diminishing. The Census Records show that in 1841, four years after the start of Victoria's reign, the population of Totnes stood at 3,049 persons, it increased shortly afterwards to 3,828 but at the end of Victoria's reign in 1901 it had, in overall terms, hardly grown: the total population was only 3,116. However, nearby Newton Abbot stood at a comparable 3,456 persons in 1841 but sixty years later it had grown to 10,738.[2] Totnes also does not compare favourably with some of its other neighbours:

the economies of nearby coastal towns Teignmouth and Torquay were greatly boosted by tourism but Totnes was not able to compete with the attractions of the seaside. Instead, in its character it was more like most other small inland towns, such as Ashburton, Modbury or South Molton, which at best were able to maintain their populations but generally lost rather than gained. Victorian Totnes was, like many others in nineteenth-century Devon, a 'sleepy' market town.

Certainly there was a constancy in the affairs of the Church of England in Totnes: one man, James Walrond Burrough, was vicar at St Mary's church from 1838 to 1888, in effect 50 of Victoria's long reign of 64 years. The previous incumbent, Joseph Cuming, was there nearly as long; he was at Totnes from 1795 to 1838. It appears Burroughs was responsible even for the church not being decorated at Christmas for half of the nineteenth century.

For those interested in Totnes the reports show the

minutiae of local life which can be both fascinating and informative. These glimpses into the lives of strangers long dead embellish our understanding of the town and add yet another facet to the rich and diverse character of Totnes.

[1] Percy Russell, *The Good Town of Totnes (Exeter, 1963)*, 90-92.

[2] I am grateful to Mr Philip Carter for this information from his University of Exeter MA thesis on the growth of Newton Abbot in the nineteenth century.

VICTORIAN
NEWS
from
TOTNES

June 23 1838

Coronation festivities – Five splendid oxen costing about £25 each, have been purchased with the cash sent by the Duke of Somerset, Lord Seymour and Mr Parrot, which are to be driven through Totnes and Bridgetown, on the 25th instant, preceded by music &c., then killed and afterwards distributed amongst the poor in proportion to the size of their families on the day of the coronation. The reformers [will then] dine together on the castle green, a band will be in attendance and all sorts of amusements introduced. In the evening the liberals are to have a ball at the Assembly Room in the Mayoralty

House, which is expected will be very fully attended. We do not hear that Sir George Adams (the unsuccessful candidate at the last election who then professed himself to be the poor man's friend by voting for the repeal of the Poor Law Amendment Act, provided he were returned as one of their representatives) or any other of the leading conservatives have subscribed [money] in order to give to the families of the poor of this borough.

June 30 1838

Our arrangements were published last week fully. The provisions for the poor were duly apportioned by the committee; the beef having been supplied by Messrs Searle and Carter. A good dinner was given to the poor in the workhouse, of roast beef and plum pudding, with a quart of strong beer per man, and a pint for each woman, with tea in the afternoon.

A dinner for the charity children &c was given under the

direction of Mr Bovey, at the Shambles Gate. There was a service in the church, and the able choir gave the Coronation anthem with good effect.

The morning was ushered in with the firing of a salute of cannons, which thundered forth at daybreak from the old ramparts of the ancient castle. The bells struck up simultaneously, and other general festivity awakened throughout the town. The Harberton liberal band, which had been engaged by the committee, was led off by their melodious chief, Mr Treeby. The Totnes band would have been engaged if they had been considered fit for their work, but as they have been touched in the wind by their hard blowing in the cause of the Tories, it was feared that they would not have wind enough left for a loyal day's work, and so the committee availed themselves of the Harberton band. Shops were generally closed, and the day was spent with much hilarity – but the differences between reformers and Tories were not abandoned even on this festive occasion.

The Tories are charged with having in this borough, as in other places, thrown cold water on the preparations for the general festivity, and we are assured that they entered into it rather reluctantly than otherwise. As however they form literally, and in fact a miserable minority, they had not power enough to disturb the general joy of the day.

In the afternoon, at two o'clock, the reformers dined together in the beautiful Castle Green, under the shade of those splendid elms, and they made the merry green wood ring with their festive mirth...

As soon as the cloth was removed, the gates were thrown wide open for the general admission of the public; and on the health of her Majesty being proposed, the enthusiasm of the company was greater than any we had ever before witnessed. The company sprung up from their seats as one man, and the cheering was echoed and re-echoed like the thunder itself. The other loyal and constitutional toasts were well received, and the day was spent in the greater harmony.

In the course of the afternoon dancing on the green, and other rustic sports took place. The leading part of the company adjourned in the evening to the assembly room at the mayoralty house where the ladies were duly honoured, and the merry dance was kept up, with all its mystic mazes, till an early hour this morning. The utmost order and regularity prevailed, under the direction of the stewards, to whom the greatest credit is due for their gentlemanly attention to the comforts of the party – more especially the ladies, whose right to the honour of the evening was acknowledged with redoubled zeal, on account of the occasion – the South hammers, at all times gallantly devoted to their duties, were on the present occasion doubly zealous to show their devotion to the sex which has supplied the nation with a monarch; and the attention generally paid to the ladies was acknowledged in terms of the highest satisfaction by the dear creatures themselves...

A portion of the Tories assembled in a shed behind the walls which was suitable to their backward state and disloyal fancies. The place, for room it cannot be called, was a shed appropriated by Mr Bentall to the drying of his serges, and in this sergery they were very appropriately accommodated, being sick at heart, and only rejoicing like men in a state of melancholy merriment. It is a rough and uncouth looking place, full of tenter hooks, commonly called rack hooks, and just such a place as a fellow sick of this world would choose to hang himself in – we hope that no coroner's inquest will follow this merriment. The Tories being unable to get up a ball for the younger ladies, gave a tea party to the elderly ladies at Lady Elford's...

September 22 1838

On Monday, the 17th, there being a large vessel to be launched at Dartmouth, the Dart steamer took some 150 persons from Totnes to witness it, returning in the evening. The landing of the passengers, and the large assemblage who had waited for her return, whilst the band was playing on the

Plains, set the lower part of the town quite alive. The company were quite delighted with the launch, and the pleasantness of the excursion. The steamer makes an expedition to the Start in a few days.

November 17 1838

On Friday week some youths having an old turned coat and some other old clothes, manufactured them into something in shape like a man, carried it about the town, and exhibited it with lighted torches, and finally burned it in the Ashburton road, conjecture was all afloat as to who it was intended for, and at length it was generally agreed that it meant no other person than a certain renegade poetaster [a would-be poet or rhymester] living not a hundred miles from the fish market.

December 1 1838

In consequence of the uncommonly heavy rain, the river Dart rose last evening to so great a height, that the lower part of the town, the Plains, Warland, &c, were completely inundated, and this afternoon it rose again to nearly the same height, the passengers and their luggage going by the Subscription coach to Plymouth were taken in a hand cart from the [Seven] Stars door, some way up the street, where the coach had stopped, yesterday a quantity of timber was seen floating down the stream and several sheep; the wind is blowing quite a hurricane, but we have not heard of any damage done.

August 25 1840

On Sunday afternoon last, between two and three o'clock in the afternoon, some hundreds of persons were assembled at the Weir, near the Race Course, a report having been circulated that some persons calling themselves Baptists were to be dipped; after waiting some time, four persons made their appearance, two females and two males, who immediately walked into the water up to their waists, when one of the males, who appeared to be a preacher, gave the others a good ducking. They remained in the water upwards of ten minutes; they then came on shore and after having changed their clothes, a sermon was preached to the persons assembled to witness the dipping. It was rumored that the parties came from Torquay.

December 5 1843

A preliminary meeting of the Totnes Agricultural Association (which is intended to be established at Totnes, on Tuesday next at Sawyer's Castle Inn, to be called the Totnes Association) was held at the offices of Messrs Edwards and Bryett.

June 24 1845

Mr Cooke and his equestrian troop made a grand entree into this town on Saturday. The bills stated they would arrive at twelve o'clock, and before that time the streets were lined with spectators. At half-past twelve the equipage made its appearance, Mr W. Cooke driving ten splendid horses in hand, and he certainly handled the ribbons very dexterously. The performances came off in a field belonging to Mr Webb, of the Seven Stars, Totnes, and gave general satisfaction.

July 22 1845

A lecture on Temperance and Total Abstinence was delivered at the Guildhall, Totnes, by a Mr Treleaven, on Wednesday the 16th instant.

Messrs. Batty and White's collection of wild beasts and their stud of horses will perform in Totnes on Thursday next; fourteen horses will be driven in hand by Mr Bulzer, and no doubt the sight-seeing folk of Totnes and its vicinity will patronize this first rate troupe.

At the Guildhall on Tuesday, Jane Avent, alias Long Tom, a lady of the pave, was brought up to answer the complaint of a man named Tippet, who had got her taken into custody by alleging that she had stolen two five pound notes. The prosecutor, having been called three times and not appearing, Avent was discharged. A man named Farley was summoned to appear against her, and in leaving the court, she politely gave him a kick in an unmentionable place, and on coming into the open air she administered a second dose in the shape of a box under the ear, with an intimation that if ever he came near her residence he would be favoured with a *quantum suff* [as much as would be sufficient].

January 4 1847

On Thursday the Totnes Reform Band attended the opening of the Railroad to Newton [Abbot], taking with them some of the Reform Banners, which have floated so many times in the cause at Totnes, Dartmouth and elsewhere, one of which was most appropriate, 'The Effect of Perseverance' which was carried in procession through the town before the managers. The weather was good, and everything passed off well. About

40 sat down to a late dinner at the Globe Hotel, where the band also attended, and gave, during the repast, some splendid specimens of their perseverance.

January 11 1847

On Christmas Eve, or rather on the morning of Christmas Day, as the Reform Band, who had visited the houses of the neighbouring gentlemen, particularly the Reverend Chancellor Martin at Harberton, and Jasper Parrott, Esquire, at Dundridge (where their abilities were duly appreciated), were returning to exhilarate the townspeople, a desperate and violent attack was made on them by some of the Tory Band, particularly by Henry Bartlett, junior, and George Bartlett – the latter of whom, without any provocation, completely blackened the eyes of Hannaford, the trumpet player in the Reform Band, and assaulted Evens, one of the buglers, for which two summons were issued against the latter, and one against the former.

And Saturday they appeared at the Guildhall before John Derry, Esquire, Mayor, and other magistrates to answer the complaint. Mr W. F. Windeatt appeared to protect the Reformers from the many similar attacks that have been made on them, by their rivals, who jealous of their transcendent abilities, and not being able to play them down, endeavour to put them down by brute force. At Mr Windeatt's instigation the affair was settled out of court by the Bartletts promising never to repeat these insults and to pay all the expenses incurred.

January 18 1847

The Totnes new market has been commenced by the building of a wall, under the supervision of Mr S. Cuming, the market surveyor, the whole length of the premises occupied in front by Mr W. Coaker, draper, and further back by Mr Toope, plasterer, the house lately occupied by Mr John Taylor, bookseller, &c, is nearly demolished...

April 12 1847

A few days ago, Mr Prowse of Totnes, dairyman, fell from a loft near fifteen feet high, and being a very weighty man, injured himself so that he now lies in a very precarious state.

April 26 1847

The railroad is in rapid progress, the permanent rails are laid, very near, and the electric telegraph quite to Totnes mill leat; the station house is commenced and from the number of hands at work on it, will soon be completed, and it appears there is no impediment to the line being shortly opened to Totnes.

The new market, which a short time ago was progressing very steadily, but now by some unaccountable reason (at least so public) a part of the work, particularly that part which was to be appropriated to the sale of fish, and was roofed so far in advance as to be ready for slating, is taken down, and a portion of that wall in the front of the street is shortly to follow.

December 28 1847

Totnes Mechanics Institute – On Tuesday evening last the Reverend W. Tarbotton of Totnes delivered a lecture on 'Fortune Telling' before the members of this Institution. There was a large attendance of members and the novelty of the lecture attracted also a great number of non-members.

January 8 1848

On Christmas Day the inmates of the Union House were regaled with a substantial dinner, plum puddings, &c, they were also allowed a pint of mild beer, and one pint of strong, to make themselves as cheerful as they could at this festive season.

The Town Council have ordered their surveyor, Mr S. Cuming, to thoroughly investigate the state of the town so far as its cleanliness is concerned, and it is generally believed, that they will use active measures to remove many of those inducements to contagion which unfortunately, too plentifully exist in the back parts of the town. Should they do this, it will indeed be a praiseworthy thing, for too many remember the sad havoc the cholera made, when last here, and we cannot of course expect to be made exempt, if cleanliness is not resorted to.

It has been a subject of general remark, that the roads in and around Totnes, are allowed to be in a dreadful state, as far as the accumulation of mud is concerned; this is too plainly exemplified in the road and pathway to the railway station, which is really in a disgraceful plight, from the want of an occasional scraping. It is to be hoped that this will not be overlooked, and that the proper authorities will continue to enforce the sanitary measure they have begun to adopt.

The celebrated Totnes brass band played many beautiful compositions from Handel, and other masters, on the Plains, on the afternoon of Christmas Day. The weather being very fine, a large concourse of people assembled, to enjoy their dulcet strains, this may be justly esteemed one of the finest amateur bands in the west.

July 9 1852

The nomination [for the Parliamentary election] took place on Wednesday. At an early hour the electioneering spirit was manifested throughout the town, by means of the principal houses being decorated with flags and evergreens. Electors and non-electors were eager in preparing for the struggle, and the only topic prevailing amongst them was the result of the election. The Tories seemed to bewail themselves on their deplorable condition, and although they mustered a band of music, and a few flags, the number of respectable persons who accompanied them were 'few and far between'.

On the other, the flags belonging to Mr Mills, the new candidate, were of the most exquisite description, and presented a striking contrast to the worn-out and scanty few of the Tories. The number and respectability of the electors who accompanied the honorary gentlemen completely cast the opposite party into the shade. At eleven o'clock a thousand persons had congregated near the hustings, which were erected on the area opposite Webb's Hotel and on the candidates ascending the hustings they were vociferously cheered by their friends...

July 16 1852

Lord Seymour and Mr Mills were returned on Thursday last as the representatives for the borough of Totnes. The long-tried and self-styled consistent member for this borough for 26 years, and 13 years consecutively (Mr Baldwin) has been rejected by 13 votes.

February 7 1857

Stealing 'Eleven' Onions — At the Guildhall, Totnes, Monday last, before his Worship (James Gill, Esquire), Admiral Michell, and Charles Webber, Esquire, William Skinner, in the employ of Mr Presswell, town clerk of the borough, was brought up charged by him with stealing eleven onions of the value of 2d, his property. Prisoner was in his employ as gardener, groom, and to do any other work needed, for which he allowed him 11 shillings per week and vegetables. Suspecting that he was not strictly honest, he kept a watch on him and on Saturday evening called him into his office, and then bade him show the contents of his pockets, in which was proved to be found eleven onions, said to be of the value of 2d. Their worships, having consulted together, sentenced the prisoner to 14 days' hard labour at the county gaol.

June 27 1857

A Ventriloquist at fault – On Monday 1st, at the Guildhall, before J. Gill, Esquire (mayor), and a full bench of magistrates, J. Diott, a book-canvasser, was charged with obstructing the meeting at the independent chapel, on the previous evening, by attempting a game at ventriloquism (of which he is known adept), but being intoxicated failed in escaping detection. The original charge was abandoned, but the defendant was convicted for being drunk and disorderly, and fined 5 shillings, and 4 shillings 9 pence costs, which was paid.

July 4 1857

Protection of the town by night – Totnes is an almost solitary instance among towns of being left without public lights by night, or even a night policeman. This appears to give great encouragement to the burglar, for during the past month two very extensive robberies have been committed – first, at the Post Office; and secondly, at the shop of Mr E. Evens, silversmith; but still as yet the Watch Committee, a body in name only, are not convinced they have a duty to perform in making some provision for the better protection of the town by night.

July 18 1857

Hay Harvest – During the past fortnight the weather has been highly favourable for haymaking; the crop is very fine and heavy — the whole of which may now be said to be well stacked.

November 7 1857

A great number of blankets were on Tuesday last distributed to the poor of this town by the ladies belonging to the Blanket Society.

November 14 1857

The Fifth of November — The usual demonstration on the evening of this day was kept up with great spirit this year, and although there was an absence of a bonfire the other attractions were far greater than for years past. Nena Sahib, the Indian rebel and murderer [known for the Massacre of Cawnpore], came in for a full share of odium, his effigy being seated on a large carriage drawn by a horse, and chained down, whilst a female stood over him with a drawn dagger. On the Plains, when the mass had congregated, fireworks were freely let off, to the damage of sundry coats and dresses, there being a goodly sprinkling of females present. Only one accident occurred, and this to a sailor, named James Ireland, recently paid off from the *Indefatigable*, who had a pistol, intending to frighten some females, and covered the muzzle with his left hand, when it went off and shattered his hand in a shocking manner. He was taken to the Lord Nelson, and medical assistance instantly procured.

March 6 1858

Great Curiosity – On Monday last there was exhibited in this town a lamb having six legs, the property of Messrs Quints of Higher Longcombe Farm, Berry Pomeroy.

January 22 1859

On Friday next, the 28th instant, Hoffman's Organophonic

Band will give an entertainment. The performance of this band in the town is looked forward to as likely to afford a rich treat.

May 14 1859

A lad was recently charged here with stealing, and was told by the worthy magistrate that being guilty, he must do one of two things either go to prison or go and serve as a sailor on board one of H. M. ships. The prisoner was glad of such an opportunity to get free, and consented to serve Her Majesty.

July 3 1859

On Saturday last this town and neighbourhood was visited with a terrific thunderstorm, which lasted many hours. A number of sheep were killed.

July 16 1859

During the past week several otters have been seen in the river Dart.

July 23 1859

Great complaint is made by the inhabitants of the dusty state of the streets. In other towns water carts are provided.

July 30 1859

Robert Mogridge, a dairyman, had four cows killed by lightning on Saturday last. His loss has created much commiseration and a subscription is being raised for him. His cows were the principal means of support for himself and his family. T. Bryett, Esquire, of Totnes, has consented to receive subscriptions on his behalf.

September 10 1859

Shooting commenced on the 1st instant, and since then large numbers of birds have been brought down. In this neighbourhood they are strong on the wing and very plenty.

September 24 1859

On Tuesday last an accident which nearly ended fatally occurred to a young person. He was going down the street, when he was caught by a good-sized crinoline, worn by a young lady, and thrown upon the ground. It was at first supposed that he had broken his neck.

October 1 1859

Interesting Discovery – A discovery of no little interest to antiquarians has been made on the premises of Mr Heath, of the Seven Stars Hotel, Totnes. His workmen were taking down some old walls in his back yard when they found enclosed within the walls a granite doorway, the columns about 6 feet in height and spanned by an arch, also of granite. The pillars and arch are adorned with moulding and elaborate fretwork. It is remarkable that the house adjoining the yard is described in its title deeds as the 'Chantry Priest's House' and this gateway now discovered is supposed to have formed the entrance to the Priest's Chapel. But the antiquarians are not altogether decided upon this point, although they are pretty well agreed that the gateway is of the architecture of the 14th century. Mr Heath intends to erect the gateway at the entrance to his garden.

October 22 1859

There is an apple tree belonging to Mr George Godfrey, of this town, which has budded twice this season, and borne fruit each time.

Those tenants of the Duke of Somerset, who showed their independence at the last Totnes election, have received notices to quit their property they hold under his grace.

December 10 1859

We regret to say that the early closing movement is not adopted in this town.

It has been agreed by the tradesmen of this town, that as

Christmas Day falls on a Sunday, they will close their shops on the following Monday.

We are glad to state that through the instrumentality of Mr W. Oldrey, the proprietors of the river steamers plying on the Dart have agreed, in the ensuing summer, to run twice every Sunday to enable parties to visit Dartmouth and Totnes in time for services at each place, and to return. This arrangement has given great satisfaction to all persons at both places.

December 17 1859

On Wednesday last there was a fall of snow.

A great complaint is made by the public of the irregularity of the trains. In many cases they do not arrive for more than an hour after the time appointed. We hope this soon will be remedied, and also that more civility and impartiality will be shown to the public by the officials at this station.

January 21 1860

A most disastrous fire broke out about one o'clock this morning, in the wine and spirit stores of Mr Bentall, in this town. The premises are entirely destroyed, as is also the house adjoining. The Masonic Lodge, with all the insignia, was consumed and the damage is estimated at £2,000, which is partially covered by insurance.

March 17 1860

Explosion of a Locomotive and loss of life – On Tuesday, about one o'clock, the boiler of the 'Tornado' engine exploded in the goods shed, at the South Devon Railway Station. The report was heard throughout Totnes, and created considerable alarm. The Tornado had just come down from Newton [Abbot] with a luggage train; and the engine driver, Amos Hall, was about to shunt the train, when the explosion took place. He was blown into the air, and fell on a truck quite dead. Robert Rice, the stoker, was much, but it is hoped not fatally, injured. The points man, Dunsford, though close to the locomotive, escaped scathless. A large portion of the roof of the goods station was scattered in fragments to a considerable distance. Assistance was telegraphed for from Newton, and the line was quickly cleared. Rice, the stoker, after receiving every medical attention from Mr Owen and Mr Harris, of Totnes, was sent on to his home by the next train. Hall, the driver, has left a widow and two children. An inquest was opened on Wednesday, but adjourned for the attendance of a government inspector.

August 11 1860

Fete Champetre – On Wednesday last, by the kind permission of the Duke of Somerset, a fete was held within the walls of the ancient castle of Totnes, for the benefit of the Mechanics' Institute. Mr W. Hole, junior, delivered an address which was much applauded. The band of the Royal Marines was present from Plymouth, and there was much dancing. There were also Ethiopian Serenaders, Torquay Maypole dancers, archery, quoits, and other sources of amusement. The weather was not so propitious as could have been wished, but the fete was attended, and it is hoped there will be a good surplus for the funds of the Institute.

September 22 1860

Mr W. S. Woodin gave his entertainment entitled 'Olio of Oddities' at the Assembly Rooms last Thursday evening, before a large and highly delighted audience. His impersonations were remarkable, and drew forth frequent bursts of applause.

It is announced that on the 28th instant, the Totnes Minstrels will give a concert of Negro melodies, at the Mechanics' Institute. This company consists of eight respectable young men of the town. Their first public appearance in character was at the Conservative concert and ball, which took place in November last, when several of their songs were encored. The company then consisted only of five, but since that time they have an addition of three, one of whom is a clever performer on the violin. Recently they were engaged at the fete held in the Castle, when their performances were again encored.

October 27 1860

On Saturday last, the Dart Fishing Company caught a splendid salmon at the Weir Pool which weighed 20 lbs. It was seen by a great many of our townsmen in the evening and on Monday was sent to Billingsgate.

August 7 1863

As usual, at this time of year, we have had a large number of visitors for some weeks past, all of whom have expressed their admiration of the unrivalled scenery around Totnes. At the present time the country is looking delightful from the diversity of scenery here – hill and dale interspersed with rich woods and orchards, golden cornfields, and verdant pastures.

The Dart is also a great attraction, and never before were there so many pleasure boats on the river. The steamer also plies between this and Dartmouth with the utmost regularity. Great improvements are being carried out at Mrs Beazley's, Seymour Hotel, for the accommodation of visitors. The Seven Stars, Railway Hotel, and other houses are also well patronized. Some of the amateur fly fishermen have of late had capital sport, taking occasionally a salmon, or salmon peal, in addition to trout. Salmon have been plentiful, and what are termed 'harvest fish' – nice little fellows – from 4 to 6 to 7 pounds each, are now coming in, price 10d to 1 shilling per pound. Whilst 'monitors' are also caught – one a short time since nearly 40 pounds.

April 29 1864

We are happy to be able to announce that the monument to the memory of young Wills, who lost his life whilst exploring the interior of Australia will be speedily proceeded with...

October 18 1864

We are glad to be able to announce that about sixty of the principal tradesmen of the town have consented on and after the first of November next to close their places of business at seven o'clock instead of eight as now. This will be for the four months of November, December, January and February, and will be a great boon to the young persons in the various shops.

November 29 1867

The New Steamer – *The William Joseph*, steamer, will ply between this and Dartmouth during the winter. She is 142 feet long, has beautiful saloon cabins, and is very handsome. She only draws two feet of water. She is from London, where she was built a short time since, and belongs to a company formed in this town. She will lie at the side of the Bowling Green Quay, instead of at Dartmouth.

A Voice from Australia – The following is an extract

from a letter written by a Totnes man, who left that town in 1850, and finally left England for Victoria in 1863. It is dated September 1867 –

'I keenly felt the loss of so many valued friends and acquaintances in and around that corrupt borough of Totnes, yet of all the counties of England, Devonshire has supplied us with a fair quota of emigrants, for I meet with Devonshire men in every part of Victoria, and I am happy to say in almost every instance West of England men have shown themselves equal to grapple with all the difficulties that meet every emigrant on arriving in a strange country, all of them being well to do and in very many instances they have made or are making an independence. Most of the parties that I have come across are from Teignmouth, Newton, Torquay, Brixham, Dartmouth, Kingsbridge, Modbury, Buckfastleigh, Ashburton, and last, but not least, Totnes, where I had the happiness to reside for thirty years... William Curry'.

January 7 1868

Skating – During the week this pastime was actively indulged in on a large field of ice near the town. A short time since some energetic young men, fond of the art, engaged a meadow on which the water from an adjoining lake could easily be turned; consequently, they have had some two or three acres of ice in capital condition.

March 1 1872

Thanksgiving day [to mark the recovery of the Prince of Wales] at Totnes was observed as a general holiday, all the shops and places of business being closed. The Deputy Mayor, Mr Alderman Rose, and Corporation attended Divine Service at Totnes Church in the morning and the volunteers, under the command of Captain Champernowne and Lieut. Kellock, preceded by the band of the corps, playing 'God Bless the Prince of Wales', also marched to church...

June 14 1872

The boot and shoemakers of this town have formed themselves into a society, and have asked the masters for an increase. The demand has been acceded to by Mr John Tozer, one of the principal tradesmen, but the advance he has made is not considered sufficient by a certain section of the workmen. His liberality, however, has been acknowledged by a formal vote of the society men.

August 9 1872

A statement is prevalent that the amount required by the directors of the South Devon Railway Company, to construct the tramways to the Totnes Quays is promised, and that the work will be shortly commenced.

September 13 1872

Totnes & Bridgetown Races – This popular race meeting was commenced on Tuesday under favourable auspices. The rain of

Monday rendered the course in capital going order. There was a large number of booths and exhibitions the whole length of the course, which were largely patronized. The South Devon Railway Company ran excursions from Plymouth and Exeter, which brought a large number of people, but on the whole the number of spectators was under the average. There were five events on the card, but unfortunately only three of these came off, the Hunt Steeplechase and the Handicap Hurdle race falling through. Notwithstanding these drawbacks, the sports was capital, the Flying Steeplechase proving one of the most exciting races that has ever been witnessed at this old-established meeting.

The Flying course was once around the flat course, over several flights of hurdles, and a stone wall; across the river, along the marshes by the railway, taking on the way several stiff jumps. The banking course was down the flat, across the river, up the steep hill, around the quarry on the top, back down over several fields, into the turnpike road, across the river, and up the straight...

May 15 1874

May Fair – This fair was held on Wednesday, the attendance being unusually large. The supply of cattle was good, cows and cattle being plentiful. The sheep of every description was particularly fine, and trade, on the whole, brisk.

The following were the ruling prices: best beef 80s to 84s per cwt, second ditto 75s to 80s, store cattle 58s to 62s, cows and calves 60s to 65s, sheep (in wool) 8d to 9s per pound, *shorlings* [the skin of a recently shorn sheep or its wool] 7d to 8d, lambs 10d, wool 1s per pound.

Some good cart horses were in the market for sale, belonging to Mr Thomas of Plymouth. At the horse fair in the afternoon, the entire horses were exhibited on the plains, the muster being large, and the breed good in their respective classes, and attracted much attention. One of these horses, on being led out of the stalls, kicked an old man rather severely in his right thigh, after which he kicked at a horse in a cart passing at the time, also doing some slight damage.

Messrs. Widdicombe and Body, and Messrs. Ward and Chowen, held auctions for the sale of a number of well-bred rams, which realized from five to twenty guineas each. Messrs. Rendell and Symons also held auction for the sale of a variety of fat and store stock, which sold at remunerative prices.

The demand for store bullocks was not so brisk as at previous markets, in consequence of the scarcity of keep, nor was the demand for fat bullocks very great.

October 2 1874

Narrow Escape from Drowning – On Friday afternoon a man named Maddick, of Totnes, had a narrow escape from drowning. It appears he was holding a boat at St Peter's Quay, waiting for some parties to embark, when, having one foot on the quay and the other on the gunwale of the boat, the boat drifted with the tide, and he, losing his footing, fell into the river. The tide was high at the time, and there were twelve feet of water in the river at the place where he fell in. Being unable to swim he would in all probability have been drowned had not a lad named Weymouth, seeing his perilous position, jumped in and succeeded in bringing him to the shore.

January 8 1875

Miss Heath, of this town, recently wrote an acrostic on 'Prince Albert, the good', which, after having been tastefully illuminated by Mr White, of Exeter, she forwarded to Her Majesty the Queen, for her acceptance, the result of which was an acknowledgement from Lieut. General Sir T. M. Biddulph, Her Majesty's private secretary.

February 12 1875

Serious accident – Mr William Harvey, of Frogmore Farm, Ashprington, was returning from Totnes about ten o'clock on Friday night, and on arriving at a place called Ashprington Post his horse shied at a tree which had been blown down and threw his rider. Mr Harvey attempted to rise, but found that he had broken his left leg.

The place where the accident occurred is about half a mile from Mr Harvey's farm, and finding that he was unable to rise, he attempted to crawl towards his house, but the pain he suffered was so great that he was compelled to give up the attempt, and as no one passed during the night he remained in the road till about seven o'clock on Saturday morning, when he was discovered by some labouring men on their way to work.

He was then conveyed to his home, and a messenger dispatched to Mr Wallis, surgeon, of Totnes, who was quickly in attendance, and found that both bones below the knee of the left leg had been broken. He set the leg, and reports that Mr Harvey is doing well.

Strange to say, the horse did not as is usually the case, proceed to its house, but grazed in the hedges near its master until the morning.

April 2 1875

A Chain of Office for the Mayor – A very pleasing ceremony took place on Totnes on Wednesday, when a chain of office for the chief magistrate of the borough was presented to the Mayor and Corporation. The chain and its medallions cost £140, and weigh $21\frac{1}{2}$ ounces. The Mayor, Corporation, and magistrates met at the Gate House, in the afternoon, and from there marched to the Guildhall, preceded by a guard of honour, formed by about thirty members of the Totnes Rifle Volunteers. The Guildhall was densely crowded and the solicitor's box was filled with ladies....

Mr Fortescue, in making the presentation on behalf of the subscribers, referred to the fact that the chain was the work of one of the oldest tradesmen of this town. Totnes was one of the most ancient boroughs, if not the most ancient borough, in the kingdom. It was mentioned as a borough in the Domesday Book, and there was evidence of its being a walled town in the time of William the Conqueror. But it claimed a much longer antiquity than this, for it was asserted that Brutus landed there, and on the stone on which he landed he had for the first time the previous day set his foot. Mr Fortescue afterwards placed the chain around the Mayor's neck, and Mr Windeatt then presented the Mayoress with a handsome bouquet, which had been placed by the chain during Mr Fortescue's remarks.

The Mayor (Mr Jeffery Michelmore) returned thanks on behalf of the Corporation for the very handsome present, and said he hoped it might be a token of good feeling and friendship for years to come. He referred to various interesting periods in the history of the borough, and said he hoped the gift would prove an incentive to the young men aspiring for office who he then saw around him.

Mr Chaster, in moving that a record should be made of the presentation, said that since Mr Fortescue had told them they ought to be satisfied with the Conqueror, he was satisfied with him (laughter). But he thought that might go back a great deal further. The antiquity of Totnes was unquestionable, and history told them that they had descended in a direct line from the Trojans, and it was undeniable that Brutus landed at Totnes. He hoped that as the Trojans of the olden time fought the giants of old, the Trojans of the present day would meet the giants of intemperance and intolerance as the giants of the future (cheers).

Mr. T. C. Kellock seconded the motion, and suggested that the names of the subscribers should be also entered on the minutes. The procession then reformed and proceeded to the Seymour Hotel, and partook of wine with the Mayor. A banquet then took place in the evening at the Seven Stars Hotel. The company numbered about fifty…

April 16 1875

Mr Frederick Neeble, of the Theatre Royal, Exeter, together with an excellent Dramatic Company, opened for a short season at the Royal Assembly Rooms on Monday evening. A drama adapted from David Copperfield, 'Our Little Emily', was produced. The various characters were well sustained by the members of the company.

May 25 1877

On Friday afternoon the foundation stone of a new Baptist Chapel, which is to be erected at a cost of about £1,500, was laid, in the presence of a large gathering of the members of the congregation and others...

June 8 1877

Large catches of salmon have been made by the net fishermen on the Dart during the past week or two, and some good baskets of fish have been also caught by the numerous rod and line fishermen.

On Tuesday morning large catches of salmon were again made by the lessee of the Weir fishery upwards of 200 very fine fish being taken, the number netted in the first haul being over 130, said to vary in weight from 8 pounds to 15 pounds each.

June 29 1877

A fire was discovered on Monday evening on the premises of Mr W. Reeves, upholsterer, situate at the rear of Fore Street, Totnes. The flames originated in the workshop, which was totally destroyed. Adjoining was a dwelling house on one side and a few paces off, on the other side, a furniture store, whilst only a very narrow passage separated a long row of tenements mostly in the occupation of poor people.

The hose was brought to play on these premises, but the flames could not be effectually subdued before the tenement adjoining, occupied by one of Mr Reeves' men, had become ignited and the roof fell in, burning some of the furniture, more, however, being damaged by water.

The fire was somewhat got under in the course of an

hour from the time it broke out, but besides the workshop a quantity of furniture and the whole of the tools belonging to Mr Reeves and his employees were destroyed.

August 10 1877

After being in comparative darkness for about six weeks, the street lamps were last week re-lit with oil.

November 2 1877

The mayor of Totnes will preside tomorrow evening at a meeting at the Guildhall of that town, convened for the purpose of discussing the desirability of forming a Debating Society at Totnes.

December 28 1877

Mrs Hill, a widow, aged about 70, residing in High Street, died suddenly of heart disease whilst sitting in a chair on Friday evening.

Friday 1 1878

We understand that the tender of Messrs Gillett and Bland, of Croydon, has been accepted for providing the new town clock to be erected at the Gate House, the price being £125.

March 15 1878

Major Micklan, R. E., with Mr Ferris, veterinary surgeon, R. H. A., attended at the Seven Stars Hotel, Totnes, on Saturday, for the purpose of purchasing horses, from four to seven years old, for her Majesty's service. About forty horses were exhibited, mostly useful farm horses, and thirteen were purchased at prices varying from £40 to £60, at an average of about £46 each. Considering the class of animals purchased, the prices realized were rather high.

April 18 1878

It will be recollected that nearly two years since, a marine store dealer of this town, named Samuel Hill, was convicted of receiving a quantity of wool, knowing the same to have been stolen, and suffered fifteen months' imprisonment. Within the past few days, a report has been published here that whilst undergoing his sentence at Exeter, Mr Hill saw the man called Brooks, of whom the former alleged at this trial that he bought the wool but who at the time could not be found.

It is stated that Brooks was recently released from prison, and Mr Hill, with some friends, took the opportunity of seeing him, when the man made a statement in writing, exonerating Mr Hill, and further stated that he went into Cornwall just after selling the wool to the other, and did not hear of Hill's conviction for six months after. He saw him in prison at Exeter, and told one of the warders that Hill was an innocent man and ought not to be there.

July 12 1878

On Monday a serious accident happened to a man named Tozer, a mason at Totnes, while at work taking down the old church at Dartington. It appears he was standing on a scaffolding inside the building, and with a pick was demolishing the wall when he overbalanced himself, and turning completely over the wall, fell to the ground, a distance of between 20 and 30 feet.

He was picked up by some fellow-workmen and it was at first feared he was dead. Mr A. Champernowne was apprised of the accident, and he immediately had the poor fellow conveyed in his carriage to his home at Totnes, where he was attended by a surgeon, who found he had fractured his collar bone, broken two ribs, and badly bruised and cut himself about.

November 15 1878

The clock which is now fixed in the Guildhall, Totnes, has been manufactured and fixed up by Messrs. Gillet, Bland and Company, steam clock factory, Croydon. It strikes upon the hour upon a bell 3 cwt, which has the arms of the borough and 'Joseph Roe, Mayor, 1878' cast upon it. The time is shown upon two 5 feet skeleton dials of solid gun metal, with the figures and minutes bronzed and the circles gilt, glazed with patent opal glass for illuminations at night. The clock is made upon the most modern principles, and is fitted with a self-acting gas apparatus for turning the gas on and down automatically. The bell was also cast in Messrs. Gillett, Bland and Co.'s bell foundry.

August 6 1880

The guard Thompson, who was injured on Thursday evening by his head coming in contact with one of the supports of Totnes station, appeared to have talked a little yesterday morning, but last evening was still in a precarious state.

October 22 1880

There have lately been several cases of typhoid fever in this town – two or three of them fatal, but of the eight cases now in the town some of the patients are convalescent.

July 21 1882

Ann Ryan, a tramp, who stated that she lived at Plymouth, was charged before the Mayor (Mr Edward Harris) with being drunk in Fore Street the previous afternoon. Defendant pleaded guilty and was sentenced to seven days' hard labour in default of payment of a fine of ten shillings.

November 10 1882

Guy Fawkes was celebrated here on Monday night with more than usual demonstration. 'Young Totnes' met in various costumes at the Plymouth Road at 8 o'clock and with blazing torches and tar barrels marched through the town, after which displays of fireworks took place on the Plains, outside the Castle Hotel, and on the corner of the Plymouth Road. Some of the fireworks were very good, and in spite of the drenching rain, were witnessed by a large number of persons.

March 2 1883

Although the Great Western Railway Company has declined to pledge themselves to work the proposed new line from Torquay to Totnes, the project is going forward hopefully. Indeed, from this very fact the confidence of some of the more farseeing of the promoters is increased. By exercising the company's running powers over a portion of the Torquay branch, it is certain that the whole of the passenger traffic between Torquay, Brixham and Dartmouth on the one hand, and Totnes, Buckfastleigh and Ashburton on the other, may be made to pass over the new line, and a considerable percentage of the traffic to Plymouth and other towns below Totnes.

Nor is this traffic likely to be small. The circular trip from Torquay to Totnes, down the Dart, and back to Totnes, is a popular one, even while the route is circuitous, via Newton. It will be much more popular when one side of a triangle has to be traversed instead of two sides.

Ashburton too, is the center of charming inland scenery.

The market produce taken to Torquay from that district will form a large item of profitable traffic. The line is not a costly one to make, and so shrewd and solid a contractor as Mr Relf will be sure to do his work well. Only a few thousands more have to be subscribed to ensure the carrying out of the project, and it will be strange indeed if the public of the district to be benefited – which includes Plymouth – do not subscribe it.

It is inevitable that the Great Western Railway will some day utilize the line for a large portion of their through traffic, including the heavy goods traffic, avoiding the steep gradients on the present line between Totnes and Newton. When the line is thus utilized, under any fair working agreement, it must become as profitable as the Salisbury and Yeovil Line was before it was merged in the South Western system – and for the same reason.

April 27 1883

The Totnes Crows – On Friday, owing to the number of

persons unable to obtain admission to the entertainments of the previous two evenings, this clever amateur company gave their performance in aid of the Volunteer Band. It has very seldom happened in Totnes that any kind of entertainment, musical or theatrical, has caused so marked a sensation. It is the intention of the 'Crows' after the warm reception thus experienced to visit other parts of the neighbourhood and give their assistance to objects of public good.

July 6 1883

Alleged Illegal Fishing – On Wednesday, at Totnes Guildhall, before the Mayor (Mr F. Bowden) and other magistrates, *Charles Selwood*, a labourer of this town, was summoned by Robert Hill, water bailiff to the Dart Board of Conservators, for illegally taking a salmon with a gaff at the waste race of the Totnes Mills, on the 11th *ultimo*.

Mr Hacker appeared for the prosecution, and Mr E. Edmonds defended. Samuel Soper, a water bailiff, said he saw the defendant at the spot named knocking the water with a stick, and each time he struck the water witness saw a salmon, as there were only a few inches of water, the fenders having been lowered. He would not swear that he saw defendant strike the fish.

Robert Hill, another bailiff, deposed to being in company of last witness on Totnes Bridge, when they noticed Selwood in the Mill race, and saw him put a fish up the bank, which he (witness) afterwards took possession of, and found it had been gaffed. He could not swear who killed the salmon. Isaac Myers, a news-vendor and the veteran fishing guide of the Dart, was charged with assisting Selwood to commit the offence. The Bench dismissed both cases on the ground of insufficient evidence.

March 27 1885

An inquest was held on Tuesday by Mr. S. Hacker, Coroner, on the body of George McKay, master of the Charity School, who was found with his throat cut on the 4th instant. The evidence showed that McKay, who succumbed to his injuries on Monday last, had been in the Army, which he left on 1st December on a pension. He had served twelve years in India, and for a month previous to the morning on which he cut his throat had complained of pains in his head. He had been married five years and had lived happily with his wife you could not give any reason for his committing the act. Rese Williams, a sister of Mrs McKay, said deceased had been 'peculiar' since he was struck by lightning about two months since…

May 22 1885

Mr J. Currie, M.D., presided at a public meeting held on Friday at the Totnes Coffee Tavern, under the auspices of the Association for Stopping the Sale of Intoxicating Liquors on Sunday. Addresses were delivered by the deputation, the Chairman, Mr J. Kelland, the Reverend R. Bowman, and Mr

F. T. Tucker, and resolution was carried against the continuance of Sunday trading in liquor.

October 23 1885

Cottage Hospital – The Cottage Hospital, at Totnes, was formerly opened by his Grace the Duke of Somerset, K. G., Lord Lieutenant of the County, on Friday last. The institution, which is the result of the efforts of a number of ladies and gentlemen of the district contains accommodation for four adults and two children, and a room specially fitted for operations and other serious cases. The premises, which have been turned into the Hospital, was formerly a small dwelling house, and are situated on the banks of the Dart, and contiguous to the town. every appliance has been provided and the hospital is superintended by Miss E. Henderson ...

January 8 1886

A veterinary surgeon of this town, while making a post

mortem examination of a large cart-horse belonging to a local firm of millers, found in the animal's stomach a triangular-shaped stone which weighed just over 3 pounds.

February 5 1886

Mr Champernowne, chairman of the Coffee Tavern Company, presided over the annual meeting of the Company, held on Monday. The report of the directors stated that it was intended to let the tavern to a good tenant. The hall in connection with the tavern had supplied a much-needed public requirement. There was a small credit balance. Mr Barrons and Dr Jelly complained that while the hall had been let to some nigger minstrels it had been refused to the Salvation Army. An angry altercation ensued and Dr Jelly left the meeting declining again to serve on the directorate.

March 26 1886

Hostility to the medical officer — A woman has been

suffering from smallpox in the higher part of the town, and on Tuesday Mr Jelley (medical officer for the borough) ordered her clothing, bedding, &c to be destroyed. The clothing was accordingly burnt in the sheep market. Certain inhabitants in this quarter took offence at the proceedings on the ground that their homes were close by, and endeavored to prevent Dr Jelley from carrying out his task. That gentlemen however, who was furnished with a pitchfork, stood on the defensive with a policeman near at hand, and finished the work. Some stones were thrown, but beyond this no serious disturbance took place, and on Mr Jelley explaining the cause of his unpleasant work the matter ended.

June 4 1886

There is a likelihood of improved lamps being adopted in the town.

The Gas Exhibition now being held at the Coffee Tavern Hall is proving a great success.

October 29 1886

Mr S. E. Burrow of Redworth Terrance, picked primroses in his garden in full bloom on Friday morning.

April 1 1887

Tuckenhay Paper Mills, which will soon give employment to a large number of hands, are being thoroughly overhauled and new machinery laid down.

June 24th 1887

At five a.m. a merry peal was rung on the Church bells [to celebrate the Queen's Jubilee] and at 8 o'clock the Volunteer Band and Fife and Drum Band paraded the town. The Mayor gave a breakfast to the police and ringers. Captain Windeatt entertained the Volunteer Band at breakfast and Mr E. Windeatt breakfasted the Fife and Drum Band. At 10.15 the procession marched to the Parish Church, where the service was conducted by the vicar,

Reverend J. W. Burrough. An interesting procession of the representative trades and public bodies marched to the Market where it dispersed and shortly afterwards 2,000 persons partook of dinner in the Market Place. Foot races, swimming matches and other sports took place during the afternoon. In the evening the town was brilliantly illuminated and the bonfire lit at 10.30. There was also a display of fireworks and a dance on the Island. The town presented a pretty appearance, being gaily decorated. Everything went off exceedingly well, the Committee doing their work admirably.

August 12 1887

Many Totnesians are complaining of the non-stoppage of the new first, second and third class express trains on the Great Western Railway line. Both the morning (up) and evening (down) trains rush through Totnes station, although there are several persons on the platform waiting for the next trains, who would gladly travel by 'the fast third' as the new train is known by. If the train pulled up at Totnes it would prove a great boon, not only to the inhabitants, but to the hundreds of excursionists who visit the Dart, the Moor, and other districts around.

September 16 1887

A serious tricycle accident occurred at Bridgetown, Totnes, on Friday to Mr Rew, manager of the Castle Brewery, Totnes. Mr Rew is an ardent tricyclist, and proceeded to Torquay to fetch his machine, which was being repaired there. In the evening he started for home, being accompanied by Mr W. W. Eynon, head master of Hill House School, Totnes. Mr Rew was on his machine that had been repaired and Mr Eynon also rode a tricycle. All went well until Bell Hill, Bridgetown, was reached. This hill is very steep indeed. When nearing Exeter Road, Mr Rew's seat slipped, and he fell head foremost. Mr Eynon was coming behind, and the wheel of his machine came into contact with Mr Rew's saddle, with the result that he was thrown to the ground. Mr Eynon, however, only suffered a shaking. The case with Mr Rew, however, was very different. He was picked up in an unconscious state, and conveyed to the residence of Mr J. Michelmore, Pomeroy House. Dr Fraser, who resides near, was soon in attendance. He attended to Mr Rew as fast as possible, and he was afterwards taken to his home in Castle Street. Mr Rew suffers from a broken collar bone, concussion of the brain and other injuries. The sufferer, who is a native of Plymouth, and is in charge of the brewery during Mr Dobree's absence, is in a very precarious state.

March 23 1888

The work of erecting a foot-bridge at the Totnes Railway Station, which was sorely needed on account of the large amount of shunting that took place, will shortly be commenced.

April 27 1888

A successful smoking concert in connection with the funds of the Totnes Wanderers Football Club was held at the Seven Stars Assembly Room last week, the Mayor (Mr T. E. L. Lloyd) presiding. The programme was thoroughly enjoyed. The last smoking club concert in Totnes was in aid of the cricket club, and that also was a great success.

May 11 1888

The Dart Rowing Club has been re-started.

May 22 1888

The Totnes Rowing Club, the members of which have added three new pair-oared pleasure boats to their stock, will shortly hold an aquatic fete on the River Dart.

November 9 1888

Some excitement was caused on Tuesday morning by the

exploits of a runaway bullock. The animal escaped from the drover and ran down South Street. On reaching the playground of the Hill House Grammar School the animal made a rush through the doorway leading into the playground. This door which opens from a large one proved too narrow for the bullock to pass through but the force with which the animal made the attempt was sufficient to completely wedge it in. The bullock could not be got out until part of the large door had been sawn away.

December 28 1888

On Christmas Day Totnes Parish Church, under the new ministry of the Reverend B. Mills, was decorated for the first time.

March 8 1889

An inquest was held at the Plymouth Inn on Monday on the body of Miss Harriet Michelmore, of Collins Road, Totnes, who met with her death by falling down a flight of stairs at her residence on Sunday night.

April 18 1889

At the Dog Show prizes will be offered to the value of £200, entries closing on May 2nd, with Mr J. L. Winter the honorary secretary, Totnes.

April 26 1889

George Andrews, a waggoner, in the employ of Messrs Tucker and Son, was playing in a football match on the Totnes Marsh on Good Friday when his leg was broken just above the ankle.

June 21 1889

An accident has happened to a crew of the Dart Rowing Club, consisting of five young men of Totnes, named Westaway, Grute, Samuel, Tozer and Janes. The crew were about to start for a practice on the Dart in a racing gig, when the boat suddenly turning over, the occupants were precipitated into the river. All were able to swim with the exception of Tozer, and they immediately struck out for the shore. Tozer by some means got one of his feet entangled in the foot strap, but he extricated himself, and on rising he struck out for the bank, from which he was only from three to four yards. He was unable to reach it and was sinking when another member of the same club, Mr Cole, jumped in and swam to him. He managed to keep him up, but found he could not bring him to the shore. Mr Fice, another member, then jumped in and between the two they kept Tozer up until a boat arrived. He was put into the boat, and landed on the bank, where he soon recovered. Westaway dislocated his shoulder.

February 7 1890

An engine-room artificer left the North Mail when it arrived at Totnes Station on Monday morning, and went into the refreshment room. The train started for Plymouth just as he came out, and in his unsuccessful attempts to enter it, he was knocked down by the last carriage and stunned. At first it was feared that he was severely injured, and a medical man was sent for, but he soon regained consciousness, and on the doctor arriving he said he was all right, and refused to be examined. He left for his ship at Devonport by the 12.9 train.

April 3 1890

The members of the Dart Rowing Club have been presented by their President, Mr W. H. Punchard of Bourton Hall, with a handsome four-oared racing gig built by Clasper. The boat is 36 feet long, and is fitted with sliding seats and patent rowlocks.

July 11 1890

Mrs Hayman of Totnes was yesterday awarded first prize for homing Antwerp pigeons at the Royal Counties Show now being held at Winchester.

October 10 1890

Yesterday the ancient custom of beating the bounds took place. It was nine years since the ceremony was last observed.

January 9 1891

Treat at the Workhouse – The Messrs Singer gave the inmates of the Workhouse their usual New Year's treat on Tuesday under the superintendence of their agent Mr W. J. McCormack. The festivities commenced with a substantial dinner consisting of joints of beef, pork and mutton, both roasted and boiled, geese, fowls and hams, followed by a plentiful supply of plum pudding, &c, and ales and lemonade...

Dinner over, the male inmates had presents of tea, sugar, tobacco and pipes, and the females and children, tea, sugar, oranges, nuts, &c. Professor Hutchings of Torquay then gave a conjuring entertainment, which seemed to give the inmates great pleasure. By this time tea was ready and it was a treat to see the way the good things provided were disposed of.

After tea a well-arranged programme of vocal and instrumental music was gone through...

March 13 1891

Totnes people have been quite shut off from the outer world since Monday. Telegrams could only be dispatched in driblets, the telephone system broke down, trade was stagnant, no newspapers entered the town, and no letters were delivered till Wednesday evening. Even on Wednesday, after the hot rays of the sun had been fast melting the snow, vehicular traffic was still impossible, and a small army of men was employed in clearing the roofs and streets. The snow plough succeeded on Wednesday in opening railway communication between Totnes and Newton, and at four o'clock the first train since Monday left the first named town. It consisted of two engines and one carriage.

Some of the officials, who have necessarily been on duty for long continuous spells, have been sleeping in the goods train at the station. Men who have walked into the town from some distance reported the roads in many places covered even above the level of the hedges. In no case were postmen with town letters able to get to the outlying districts beyond the radius of three miles. One gentleman who arrived from Newton on the snow plough attempted to get to Plymouth on horseback, but returned after having nearly lost his horse in deep drifts three miles out.

Another pedestrian reported that the Kingsbridge mail which left Kingsbridge Road Station on Monday night was blocked, that the driver and passengers had to leave the coach, and that the horses died in the snow. Telegraph poles have been blown down in great numbers. At Harbertonford a large elm tree fell and cut through the telegraph wires. A farmer who had walked some little distance out of Totnes returned with the report that hundreds of sheep and lambs are buried in the snow. At Luscombe, on Wednesday, a farmer assisted by several labourers dug out a flock of over 80 sheep and lambs which had been completely hidden. Many of the lambs were dead, but all the sheep were alive. A good many farmers, however, warned by the threatening weather got their cattle under shelter on Monday afternoon.

Wild birds have become so tame with hunger that they have flocked into the town in large numbers – not the least of many pitiable sights. On Wednesday evening the town crier's announcement that the traffic was resumed as usual with Ashburton and Newton was hailed with no little delight. All the Post Office authorities were able to telegraph from Plymouth and Exeter.

The effect of the storm has not been so damaging as might have been expected, but several large greenhouses have fallen in by the weight of snow, and in High Street the roof of part of a dwelling house also fell in. The passengers on Monday night by the train due at Plymouth at 10 o'clock waited at the station expecting to proceed at any moment. Some fell asleep in the carriages and some made themselves as comfortable as possible in the waiting room. Others less sanguine put up at the various hotels but even the short journey that they had to make was in many cases greatly exhausting.

The Kingsbridge mail cart which should have arrived on Monday evening has not yet arrived, and there has been no train from Plymouth since 7.55 on Monday evening. Since Wednesday morning a large number of carts have been engaged removing the snow from the streets but it will take many days to do so, there being such an immense quantity, and business is almost at a standstill. The first lot of letters from Plymouth since Monday reached Totnes today, via Exeter, having been dispatched from Plymouth by the London and South Western Line to Exeter.

March 3 1893

John Faulkner was on Monday sentenced to seven days' imprisonment by Mr E. Harris at Totnes for begging at Bridgetown.

Totnes Town Council met on Tuesday evening... a lengthy report of the Public Health Committee was read, in which it was stated that a communication had been received from Mr O. S. Bartlett, Clerk to the Dartmouth and Totnes Sanitary Authority, to the effect that they had purchased a steamer as a floating hospital and the portion of expense allotted to the Borough of Totnes was £100. The old police cells had been found unsuitable for a mortuary.

March 21 1893

Before Messrs E. Harris (in the Chair) and W. M. Tollit, *John Chamberlain*, an inmate of the Totnes Workhouse, was charged with assaulting a German, named Christian Depree, another inmate, on March 15th. It appeared that Depree was snoring when in bed and because he would not cease, the prisoner got out of bed, caught him held by the collar, and struck him in the face with his fist. Philip Loby, a travelling German musician, being sworn, acted as interpreter. The Bench sentenced the prisoner to 14 days' hard labour.

December 26 1896

A fire broke out at the shop of Mr Earl, seeds-man, High Street, on Sunday but was quickly extinguished by Messrs Butler (Captain of the Fire Brigade), R. Tozer, and W. R. W. Foote, who removed the grate and a portion of the wall, behind which they discovered a large beam alight.

February 7 1899

Snow fell at Totnes for an hour on Saturday but was succeeded by rain during the night. On Sunday, however, the weather was exceptionally fine.

February 17 1899

Totnes bakers on Monday reduced the price of the eight-pound loaf from 10d to 9d.

May 30 1899

Roland Willis, son of Mr W. G. Willis, of Totnes, broke his left thigh while riding on a wooden horse on three wheels, which overturned while coming down Dorsley Hill.

June 23 1899

There was a good muster of Totnes Volunteers at the Race Marsh on Tuesday when a *feu de joie* was fired in honour of the 62nd anniversary of the Queen's accession to the Throne, and the band played the National Anthem.

June 30 1899

On the picturesque island at Totnes yesterday a capital show was held under the auspices of the Totnes Chrysanthemum and Horticultural Society. The exhibits, which were of splendid quality, were situated in two spacious marquees and they were supplemented by large displays...

July 7 1899

The Duke and Duchess of York and party arrived at Totnes from the Dartmouth steamer *Totnes Castle* about six o'clock last evening, being received by the Mayor and Corporation and officials. The local Volunteers formed a guard of honour.

The Duke of Somerset introduced the mayor (Dr Gibson) who presented an address, which expressed satisfaction at the Duke's first acquaintance with the ancient borough and its beautiful river during the time he was on the *Britannia*. The Mayor also alluded to the auspiciousness of the day, being the anniversary of the Duke and Duchess's wedding, a reference which the Duke gratefully acknowledged.

The Duke inspected the guard of honour before driving away amidst enthusiastic cheering to Ugbrooke Park.

July 28 1899

On Tuesday Totnes Workhouse children had an outing to Dartmouth through the kindness of Miss Dorothy Turnor of

Derwent Lodge. They were given dinner and tea at Millbay Cove.

January 25 1901

The mournful news of the death of her Majesty was received at Totnes with the deepest sorrow. Immediately the tenor bell at the church was tolled by Mr J. D. Manley. At the meeting of the Religious Tract Society there was a crowded attendance. The Mayor (Mr F. T. Tucker), who presided, said that they met under the shadow of a great, a personal, national sorrow, and universal sorrow. Some of them had known no other name than that of her Majesty in connection with the throne of the country. Any other meeting but that would have been postponed at once, but her Majesty was a patron of the Society, and he felt sure if she could speak she would say that God's work must go on, and His Kingdom must endure for ever.

The hymn 'O God our help in ages past' was sung and Reverend G. D. Evans offered prayer, thanking God for the

Queen's reign and her example, and praying that the King and other members of the family should receive Divine comfort in their sorrow. Reverend Knox (the deputation) also alluded to the sad event.

On Wednesday in Totnes, almost without exception, the business premises had shutters up, or blinds down, and signs of mourning were generally displayed by private residents.

January 29 1901

The services at the places of worship on Sunday were of a memorial character. At the Parish Church Revered T. H. Elliott (the Vicar) occupied the pulpit in the morning and preaching from the text 'And he died in a good old age, full of days, riches and honour' said they met under the shadow of a great loss. No Sovereign has been more deeply loved, and none had more honestly tried to do her duty than the Queen. If they revered her memory they should try to walk in her footsteps. The 'Dead March' and the *'Marche Funebre'* were played.

The Revered W. J. Betts at the Congregational Chapel took 'Blessed are the dead which die in the Lord' for his text, and said a faithful country would long dwell on the Queen's Memory with affectionate regard, and thank God for the beauty and purity of her life. The stainless integrity of her life had helped to purify the moral atmosphere in a thousand homes. The 'Dead March' was played.

At the Baptist Chapel the National Anthem was sung, and Reverend G. D. Evans' text was 'His fame was in all nations'. He said it was impossible to overestimate the Queen's influence on the home life of the nation. Only the Royal Household and the officers of State present when the stories of the awful tragedies in South Africa were laid before her could appreciate the genuiness of her anxiety, and only God knew what it cost her in the vital strength which might have otherwise been conserved for years to come. The great losses in the war and the death of the Queen would inevitably be linked together in history.

Reverend J. Currey preached at the Wesleyan Chapel from the text 'The righteous shall be in everlasting remembrance'. The 'Dead March' was played at an afternoon meeting at the Y.M.C.A.. The Mayor (Mr F. T. Tucker) presided, and Reverend G. D. Evans and Mr E. Windeatt were the speakers. Muffled peals were rung on the church bells in the morning and evening.